BLUFF YOUR WAY IN GOURMET COOKING

Joseph T. Straub

CENTENNIAL PRESS

ISBN 0-8220-2226-5
Copyright © 1990 by Centennial Press

Printed in U.S.A.
All Rights Reserved

Centennial Press, Box 82087, Lincoln, Nebraska 68501
an imprint of Cliffs Notes, Inc.

INTRODUCTION

Most people would like to claim that they're experts at something. Since everybody has to eat, cooking is a logical field to choose. With the right props, some working knowledge, and a little flash, dash, and panache, you can pass yourself off as a gourmet cook.

There are more bluffers in gourmet cooking than there are in other fields, such as accounting, law, or medicine (although those fields have their share of bluffers too). You can bluff your way in gourmet cooking without having to bother with minor details such as internships, qualifying examinations, or board certification. The cost of academic training is a real bargain, too. All you had to do was buy this book!

Gourmet cooking is a popular field for bluffers because most people believe they're connoisseurs of some type of food, whether it's the home-brewed hot sauce served at a ramshackle barbecue joint or the Duck à l'Orange prepared by the chef at the country club. Nobody likes to admit to gastronomic illiteracy, but good food is, uh, a matter of . . . taste. Its wonderful subjectivity makes gourmet cooking a safe area for bluffers.

This book isn't a cookbook; it won't make you an executive chef. What it will do, with a little dedication and showmanship on your part, is help you bluff your way from the kitchen to the dining room in style. You'll learn how to fake it in a field that's already crowded

with bluffers but has plenty of room for one more.
Welcome aboard.

COME INTO MY KITCHEN

Cutlery

Every bluffer-gourmet needs a dramatic array of cutlery. You may not use it much, but it sure looks impressive sitting on your kitchen counter. The most eye-catching cutlery sets contain a matched set of chef's knives in a massive block of wood with slots for the different blade widths. The storage block fairly bristles with knife handles and makes an unequivocal statement about your prowess as a gourmet cook.

Your cutlery assortment should include a heavy-bladed **French chef's knife** (for heavy chopping, slicing, and dicing); a **utility knife** (shaped like the chef's knife, only smaller); a **paring knife** (for peeling and sculpting fruits and vegetables, fluting mushrooms, and opening the mail); a thin-bladed **boning,** or **filet knife;** a long-bladed **slicing knife;** and a **meat cleaver** for heavy-duty cutting and hacking through chicken bones.

Discriminating bluffers should insist on knives with a full tang. That means the metal of the blade extends all the way through the handle. The handle material sandwiches the metal blade, which is fully visible on the top. Full-tang knife manufacturers don't skimp on materials and usually don't skimp on quality either. Brand names such as **Henckels** and **Trident** are good ones to remember, although others, most notably

Gerber (which has nothing to do with the baby food company), have metal handles that are cast as an integral part of the blade. Beware of cheap ripoffs made of Toledo steel. Toledo, Ohio, that is.

On the practical side, you'll need some cutlery that's built for go, not for show. Start with a mail-order **Ginsu** knife set (sometimes advertised on late-night TV when the air time's cheap). You can hack away with a Ginsu to your heart's content without worrying about nicking the blade of one of those $100 full-tang, high-carbon, stainless steel knives stored in the wooden block on your counter. If the Ginsu nicks or breaks, you can replace it for less than $5, plus postage and handling.

You'll also need something that's built for flat-out speed—an electric knife. There are lots of brands to choose from, and most of them will saw their way through bread, top sirloin, or your solid mahogany dining room tabletop and barely miss a lick. They're also good for trimming shrubbery.

Round out your working set of cutlery with a machete (good for lopping sirloin steaks off a quarter of beef) and a chain saw (good for cutting up an entire steer). Electric models won't fill your kitchen with nauseating exhaust fumes and asphyxiate your dinner guests. Last but not least, consider investing in a switchblade knife. This is handy for defending yourself against muggers in the supermarket parking lot.

But how to keep all this hardware sharp? Professional chefs disdain electric sharpeners because they grind away too much expensive steel. This means that the built-in knife sharpener on the back of your trusty Rival can opener is a no-no; it won't impress anyone.

What will (and get you some approving smiles and fawning glances) is a professional chef's sharpening stone. Perhaps the most impressive, made by **Norton Abrasives**, is a three-stone set mounted in a no-nonsense, heavy black case. The grits range from coarse to very fine, and the stones are attached to a rotating device so you can select the stone you want and start whetting away. No genuine bluffer (is that a contradiction in terms?) should be without one. It's the ultimate compliment to your fine cutlery display. As for the Ginsu and machete, sharpen them on the grinding wheel at your nearest full-service gas station. Replace the chain on your chain saw according to the manufacturer's instructions.

Hand-Held Utensils

Check the housewares department at your nearby K-mart, and you'll see that you can spend a fortune on kitchen doodads so specialized that they're hardly worth taking the time to use, wash, and put away afterward. ("Honey, have you seen our digital, metric, self-adjusting egg slicer? Aw, the hell with it – gimme the paring knife.")

Several utensils are considered standard equipment for any gourmet kitchen, though, and you'd better be prepared to buy them. They are:

Assorted wire whisks Whisks can range from something tiny that will scramble an egg in a teacup to a 3-foot-tall monster that you can use to stir a cauldron full of soup – or cement. Buy several different sizes.

Nutmeg grater This shows that you're a purist. None of that preground stuff for you. Some graters have a little compartment in the top where you can store a whole nutmeg for future use. You'll look especially professional as you whip it out and rasp a few flakes of nutmeg on the egg nog and bourbon at your Christmas party.

Meat mallet This is one of the most important, all-purpose kitchen utensils. With this handy device, paranoid schizophrenics can convert round steak into filet mignon or, with a little extra effort, hamburger. Tenderizing steak with a meat mallet is in-house therapy: you can work off your resentment about slaving over a hot stove while your ungrateful guests sit around the pool drinking your booze. A meat mallet also serves as a reasonably good hammer (watch your fingers!); it's handy too for adjusting your television set when the tuner goes on the blink. Just wham the side of the cabinet a few times. If you don't have a mallet but you want to make a tough slab of beef melt-in-your-mouth tender, try backing over it several times in a car equipped with tire chains. The result's the same.

Spaghetti hook With this utensil, everyone can come by the stove and serve themselves buffet style. It beats the heck out of draining the pasta through a colander because colanders are a pain in the neck to wash. If you don't have a spaghetti hook, try a back scratcher.

Small Appliances

These, like your cutlery and hand-held utensils, communicate a lot about your savvy in the kitchen. If you're bluffing on a tight budget, buy a **blender** first. It's the most versatile appliance of all. Use it to convert mistakes into "secret sauces" and leftover salads into nourishing vegetarian cocktails. Blender owners never need to worry about lumpy gravy or sauces ever again. Ten seconds on "frappé" usually makes anything – short of roofing nails – smooth and creamy. If you don't have a blender, a garbage disposal with a drain plug in the bottom works just as well. Sterilize it first with boiling water.

Most blender models have a panel of buttons marked "chop," "whip," "grind," "purée," and so forth. The difference from one to the next is just a few hundred RPMs, which is hardly a big deal. All the buttons look impressive, though; they'd intimidate even a NASA launch technician. If you want to keep things simple, however, buy a humble two-speed model with settings for "low" and "high." I feel a psychic bond with the two-speed Hamilton Beach that I bought on a Gulf Oil Company credit card in 1966. It whines like a banshee, weighs a ton, and hasn't worn out yet. If the company could guarantee similar durability with its other products, maybe it ought to consider expanding its line a bit. Cars would be a good place to start.

You should also have a battery-powered **spice grinder** to do small jobs, such as blending spices for chili or spaghetti sauce. This adds a bit of flair to your cooking, and the sound will attract your guests' attention when you snap it on. A spice grinder is also handy for grinding small amounts of coffee. Buy the beans whole and grind only enough for one pot at a time to ensure maximum freshness. Beforehand, be sure to wipe the grinder clean of any spice residue. Otherwise, be ready to explain in your best authoritarian manner why your coffee tastes slightly like coriander, chili powder, or cumin.

You might also want to invest in a **food processor;** they seem to be standard equipment today. Actually, though, a food processor is just a blender that's been to France, and most of them have such a diabolical design that they're razor-sharp nightmares to wash and dry. More than likely, you'll probably decide to chop up your onions in your trusty blender when nobody's looking. A food processor is all right for mixing small amounts of dough, however, and if you have skeptics in the crowd, you may want to trot out your food processor and play with the "pulse" button at least once. The fastest way to wash it is to fill it with hot water and detergent and let it run for thirty seconds or so.

If a recipe calls for slow cooking, nothing beats a **crock pot.** This is the ultimate for making soups, stews, chili, or anything else that has to simmer for several hours.

Sooner or later you'll also be obliged to buy a **mixer,** and when it comes to mixers with a mind-boggling array of features, KitchenAid has practically cornered the market. Their best model has enough attachments to fill a walk-in closet. There's a rumor going around that the company is developing a limited-edition "Turbo" model with racing stripes, a Roto-Rooter attachment, a compass, and a secret compartment. The biggest one is as powerful as most compact cars and only slightly more expensive. They come in several colors, including cobalt blue and traditional white.

Last but not least, round out your array of small

appliances with a reliable **fire extinguisher.** It'll come in handy for chasing nosy guests out of the kitchen, and if the unthinkable happens and your flambé becomes a fiasco, it's comforting to have one of these nearby. Don't say I didn't warn you.

Major Appliances

Major appliances make a major statement about your legitimacy as a gourmet cook. Outfit yourself with the best equipment, and people will assume the best about your abilities. Your image is at stake here.

Ask around and you'll probably discover that the Jenn-Air **kitchen ranges** have the best press. This isn't to say they're necessarily the best, but they do look the part. They aren't sold at your typical appliance store; in fact, you may have only a handful of dealers in a metropolitan area. But they're worth looking for; the Jenn-Air's array of features (including interchangeable plug-in range-top units) is *very* impressive. You can swap griddles for grills, grills for burners, and lots of other combinations.

As long as we're talking kitchen ranges here, we probably should acknowledge a related area: gas versus electric heat. Purists who want absolute, infinite control over cooking temperatures will settle for nothing but gas. It's standard for every restaurant kitchen. Burners reach the desired heat instantly, with no warmup or cool-down time. If your kitchen already has gas, fine. If it doesn't, and if you intend to carry your bluff to the hilt, arrange to have a bottled gas (liquid petroleum gas) tank installed and run a line to your Jenn-Air kitchen range. Afterward you can brag to your guests about the extent of your dedication and your determination to control cooking heat to the nth degree. Literally.

A second major appliance, your **dishwasher,** further enhances your gourmet image. KitchenAid comes to the rescue once again. They've got a dishwasher that's considered to be the ultimate – just like their mixers. Maybe in the near future they'll offer a dishwasher attachment on one of their mixers. Or a mixer attachment on their dishwashers. Don't laugh; it's possible. Anyhow, you'll need a reliable, no-nonsense dishwasher to help your long-suffering maid (you) clean up the inevitable messes that you're destined to make, and KitchenAid has an image that complements your own. Or, at least, the one you'd like to have.

Last on the list is a **kitchen sink.** I'm not talking your standard double sink with a disposal in one side, either. I'm talking Elkay. If you haven't heard of this brand, watch TV's Jeff Smith (a.k.a. the Frugal Gourmet). Elkay is one of the companies that sponsor his show, just like Budweiser beer and Copenhagen snuff sponsor stock car racers. Don't look for Jeff to show up some Saturday morning in a "Team Elkay" jacket, though. Too unsophisticated.

Elkay promotes their sinks, faucets, and accessories to gourmet cooks with the slogan "The state of the art in the cooking arts." The sinks have several different compartments for washing, draining, and so forth, and their Eurostyle Calais faucet is something to behold. An Elkay sink is the perfect companion appliance to your gas-fired Jenn-Air range and Kitchen-Aid dishwasher.

Gourmet Gadgets

Here's where you can really wheel and deal. Perhaps the ultimate proof that you've scored major points with your guests is when one of them points to a gizmo on your counter and asks, "What's that?"

There are about as many exotic accessories as there are bluffer-gourmets, so you've got lots of gadgets to choose from. I'll keep the list small here, but if you feel you need to add a few things, just drop by any pot-pourri-scented gourmet shop and browse around for a few minutes. You'll find plenty of weird-looking gimmicks to spend your money on.

One of the most impressive accessories is a **pasta machine.** Make sure to buy one that's made in Italy and comes in a box with instructions written in Italian on the outside. Save the box and leave it in plain sight, of course.

The typical pasta machine looks like a miniature chrome mimeograph machine. It can be adjusted to crank out several widths of pasta—from lasagna to vermicelli. You might never use it, of course, but it's a good conversation piece for your kitchen. When you have a pasta dinner, the simplest thing to do is buy the stuff ready-made, like people have been doing for generations. Just be sure to hide the box. If you actually do decide to crank out a batch of homemade pasta, call the foreign language department of a nearby college first and make an appointment with a professor of Italian who can interpret your pasta machine's instructions for you.

A pasta machine naturally calls for a **pasta drying rack.** The stuff literally has to be hung up to dry after

13

it's made. If you can't find one of these, borrow a secretary's paper-collating rack from the office. It'll work just as well—maybe better.

One of the cheapest accessories, and the hallmark of dedicated bluffers and certified executive chefs alike, is an **instant-read thermometer.** This official-looking instrument resembles a long nail with a numbered dial at the top, and it's stored in a heat-resistant tube that clips to the pocket of your chef's tunic. They come in several heat ranges. Whip yours out with professional flair to check the temperature of sauces, cooking oil, or a friend's date who happens to wander into the kitchen.

Finally, consider buying a **wine-tasting cup** with a neck chain. This is useful for sampling various wines in your kitchen and for measuring and pouring them into whatever it is you've got simmering on the stove. Cooking can be a lonely job sometimes, so you may end up sampling wine a *lot* while you're waiting for the sauce to thicken or the cooking oil to come up to the proper heat.

Herbs and Spices

These can do more for a bluffer's reputation than just about anything. They look intriguing, smell unusual, and bewilder lots of people from the meat-and-potatoes school of cooking, whose idea of creativity is to add another 1/8 teaspoon of black pepper to Campbell's cream of mushroom soup. If it weren't for herbs and spices, food would taste awfully dull, and lots of chefs would be looking for other work.

It helps to know the difference between herbs and spices in case some know-it-all calls your hand. Herbs tend to be soft and succulent seed plants that don't develop a woody texture – parsley, sage, rosemary, and thyme (to quote a line from an old Simon and Garfunkel song). Spices, on the other hand, are aromatic vegetable products, such as pepper, nutmeg, and cloves. Herbs give food a rather exotic, offbeat, hard-to-pin-down taste, while spices tend to smell good and give dishes a pungent flavor. If you want to appear mysterious and secretive, always put herbs in your recipes and refuse to divulge what they are. As a bluffer, you ought to steer clear of the technicalities whenever possible and just refer to both herbs *and* spices as "seasonings." Colonel Sanders Kentucky Fried Chicken claims there are eleven different herbs and spices in the fried chicken breading, and they don't split hairs about which is which, either.

Garlic, one of the most universal seasonings, is a mainstay in salad dressings, barbecue sauces, Italian and Tex-Mex recipes, and other dishes that use lots of tomato products. You can buy it puréed in small jars, which is the ultimate in convenience, but purists insist on buying whole bulbs and crushing the cloves with the side of a chef's knife and mincing them fine. Never but *never* use a garlic press.

You'll probably want to buy a braided wreath of whole garlic bulbs in a gourmet food store and hang it up on the wall to use as needed. A garlic garland adds a lot to your kitchen's atmosphere (pun intended) and wards off vampires. Chew a clove while you cook to drive away kibitzers who stroll into the kitchen and ask unwelcome questions, such as "When's dinner?" or

"Do I smell something burning?" The odor of fresh garlic on your breath will knock a buzzard off a garbage truck.

A string of sun-dried, crimson chili peppers also adds a sassy Southwestern touch to your kitchen. Like the garlic wreaths, they can be found in gourmet shops or purchased from mail-order catalogs. Be sure not to rub your eyes after handling them. If you do, you'll feel like you just stuck your face into a blast furnace.

Bluffers should make a big point of emphasizing that it's the seeds and ribs inside these chilies that incinerate everything south of your uvula – not the meat of the pepper itself. You know better. If a person wanted to create infernal internal combustion, he'd soak the chilies in water to reconstitute them and then use them *whole*.

In addition to garlic and chilies, an earthenware bowl of gourds adds a pleasant, peasanty touch. They're sold around Thanksgiving in lots of supermarkets, and if properly dried, they'll last for months.

Your working inventory of herbs and spices will be quite different from the window-dressing items mentioned above. A well-equipped bluffer should lay in a supply of such basic items as allspice, sweet basil, bay leaves, cayenne, chili powder, cinnamon, cloves, cumin, curry powder, ginger, nutmeg, oregano, paprika, rosemary, sage, sesame seeds, and thyme. These look impressive when aligned like obedient soldiers in a spice rack on your wall. Many "seasoned" gourmets prefer to blend their own "secret mix" of spices for various dishes. Experiment with the assortment listed above and see what you can come up with. If the food tastes so bad your dog won't eat it, you can always order out for pizza.

Although a spice grinder is convenient for grinding dried seasonings, some purists insist on grinding the flakes between the heel of one hand and the palm of the other—a poor person's mortar and pestle. A punster pal of mine usually does this while wailing in a falsetto voice, " 'Do it to me *rosemary*,' said *sweet basil*, . . . 'if you've got the *thyme!*' " If his humor won't kill your appetite, his cooking will.

Although many herbs are normally used in dry form, several (ginger, sweet basil, thyme, and rosemary, for example) are at their best when used fresh. That means you should consider an herb garden in a kitchen window planter. This agricultural experiment will further impress your guests and prove that you're a purist who's fanatical about having everything *exactly* right.

You can buy seeds for an herb garden in gourmet shops, of course, but they're cheaper in places like K-mart's garden shop or roadside nurseries. An herb garden can be grown inside in a well-lighted window box, in an outside window box, or in your own back yard in a plot of rich dirt. Be sure it gets plenty of water. If you plant an outside herb garden, watch carefully to be sure your neighbor's cat doesn't mistake it for a litter box. And if only weeds come up, don't worry. Nobody will know the difference.

Cooking Utensils

It's possible to stock an array of utensils large enough to fill a warehouse, so you're going to have to use some discretion here. After all, your space (and perhaps your budget) is limited. You'll naturally need a basic assortment of such pedestrian items as sauce pans, skillets, and cooking pots, but a few additional items will round out your equipment and your reputation alike.

Double boiler This is a must for making perfect sauces and melting expensive chocolate. The contents never come in contact with direct heat, so there's no danger of scorching or burning.

Wok A necessary utensil for stir-frying Chinese or Japanese foods and for soaking your feet after standing over a hot stove all day.

Pressure cooker This reinforced cooking pot accelerates cooking time considerably. It's also a lifesaver when you're running late. Be sure to follow the directions about pressure buildup and heat control, though, or you'll be inviting your guests to dine off the kitchen ceiling. Pressure cookers have a legendary ability to tame the toughest cuts of meat. They'll tenderize a '57 Cadillac bumper in an hour.

Stock pot This heavy metal pot, about one and one-half to two feet tall, is used to convert meat and poultry carcasses into rich broths to use later in soups or sauces. Simmer the bones and meat scraps, along with water and seasonings, for several hours. Then strain the liquid through some cheesecloth (a dish towel works just as well) and freeze the stock in a tightly closed container. Some stock pots have a spigot at the bottom to draw off the liquid; these are also good for mixing purple passion and serving it to a party of 50 or more. Everybody can help themselves. Just be sure you have several cabs standing by to drive everybody home.

Colander Use this holey utensil for draining things like cooked fruits, vegetables, or pasta. In an emergency, you can substitute your tennis racquet or plastic mesh fishing hat with the Peterbilt logo on the front.

THE PRESENTATION –
DAZZLE 'EM WITH
FOOTWORK

Eating is an aesthetic as well as a nourishing activity, and most of the senses are involved. The most obvious, of course, are taste and smell, but we can't overlook sight, and that's where your appearance – or more correctly, the appearance of your *food* – plays a major role. Chefs call this the "presentation," and a flashy presentation can go far toward defusing many guests' complaints – short of throwing up.

First of all, try to follow the recipes exactly. Only true gourmets should feel free to improvise. As a bluffer, too much improvisation can get you into trouble. If the food's undercooked, overcooked, or improperly seasoned, you'll have a strike or two against you. It won't taste or smell as good as it should.

Presentation is an art. Like the frame on a photograph or a painting, it should complement each course and make the food look better than it would, say, on a paper plate or on a metal tray in an Army chow line. The most basic starting point for a 4-star presentation is to arrange the items attractively. Try to keep sauces or liquids from running together. That's supposed to happen *after* the food's been eaten. Use sauce boats to prevent this catastrophe.

Position the food neatly on serving plates. Avoid

splatters and dribblings onto the tablecloth. Watch how the chefs on television deftly wipe up errant sauce trails with a lightning-quick swipe of a dish towel. What you want is an immaculate, well-defined, neatly arranged serving plate to "present" to your guests, and when you present it, be sure the most attractive parts of the food are facing them. A final nicety: warm the plates in advance for hot food, and chill them for cold food. This ensures that your presentation will arrive at the table at the precise temperature. More than one guest will probably be impressed enough to compliment you about your foresight and style.

Garnishes go far toward enhancing your presentation. It's worth your time to learn how to prepare several fancy ones.

In a free-association test, if you said "garnish" most people would reply "parsley." This isn't surprising because it's the most universal garnish of all. Nobody ever eats parsley. It's the Rodney Dangerfield of vegetables. Thus bluffer-gourmets must expand their repertoire a bit and include such things as watercress, mint, assorted fruit wedges, and carved fruits and vegetables.

Some skill at fruit and vegetable carving is important. A bouquet of fancy radish roses can impress some guests to the point that they'll ignore (or overlook) how bad the pot roast tastes. Kids will be especially impressed because they're genetically programmed to mutilate vegetables more than to eat them anyway. You can keep them occupied after dinner by allowing them to take turns throwing the carved-up vegetables down the garbage disposal. In fact, they might be willing to pay you for the privilege – a pleasant after-dinner diversion that could help offset the cost of the meal.

You'll find with a little practice that you can produce some impressive creations from such things as watermelons and cantaloupes (which can be carved into baskets) and assorted other items, including tomatoes, pineapples, mushrooms, the aforementioned radishes, green peppers, lemons, zucchini, cucumbers, and peaches. If your taste takes an erotic twist, be sure not to display X-rated work to children under 18 without parental consent. Using a paring knife and some ingenuity, you can learn to make pickles into fans, scallions into brushes, and your thumb into julienne strips if you're not careful. Lay in a good supply of Band-Aids first; you'll need them until your carving skill matures. In the meantime, if guests ask about all the little red dots on your countertop and kitchen floor, nonchalantly confess that you dropped a bottle of food coloring. Then slide your bandaged hand Napoleon-style into the front of your tunic so they won't put two and two together.

GASTRONOMIC GURUS

You should know a little about several of gourmet cooking's heaviest hitters so that you can drop a name or two when it's appropriate. These people are (or were) celebrities on the high-calorie circuit, and their names are widely known.

Jeff Smith

An ordained minister and former chaplain at the University of Puget Sound, Jeff Smith hosts his own weekly television program on PBS, called "The Frugal Gourmet." Affectionately known as "The Frug" (which reminds some people of the 60s dance), Jeff's a skinny, right jolly old elf who has almost as much fun chuckling, chortling, and chatting with his audience as he does cooking. His farewell line, "I bid you peace," makes you feel like you've been hanging out in the kitchen with your delightful ex-hippie grandfather, except your grandfather doesn't have an army of assistants to clean up after him and a slavering television crew to eat the terrific food that's just been fixed. (Ever wonder why you never get a glimpse of the crew members on television cooking shows? Probably because they're so overweight from pigging out after every show that no wide-angle lens is wide enough to encompass them in a group shot.)

Anyway, Jeff defines "frugal" as buying the best ingredients you can afford and getting the most out of them in the dishes that you cook. "Frugal" most definitely doesn't mean stingy or cheap. There's nothing cheap about the cost of some of the ingredients he puts into his mouth-watering culinary masterpieces; the studio's grocery bill probably exceeds the gross national product of some third-world countries. Luckily for us, however, Jeff has several inexpensive paperback cookbooks available, any one of which would be good to have in your cookbook library.

Paul Prudhomme

Cajun cooking has been on a roll in recent years, and the high priest of it is pudgy Paul Prudhomme. He looks like Dom DeLuise in a chef's hat. Many people credit his recipe for blackened redfish as the reason for that species' being on the endangered list. Surfers and skin-divers wish he'd blackened shark meat instead.

Prudhomme, a Louisiana Cajun, was a sharecropper's son and the youngest of 13 children. He credits his mother with teaching him most of what he knows about cooking, and his inborn love for Cajun and Creole recipes is redolent throughout his fabulously successful *Chef Paul Prudhomme's Louisiana Kitchen*. One of many unique features about this book is that he recommends substitutes for ingredients that are native to Louisiana. For example, if you can't find tasso, a specially seasoned Cajun-style ham, try Cure 81. If the butcher grunts when you ask for andouille smoked sausage, settle for Polish kielbasa.

Prudhomme's cookbook also contains copious helpful hints from his test kitchen, so bluffers, take note. There are tips on frying foods, testing oil temperatures (in your skillet, not your crankcase), making roux (which he calls Cajun napalm), and selecting various ingredients and seasonings that go into his recipes. He's often pictured seated because of the obvious effects of tasting his cooking over the years. Rumor has it that he needs a chain hoist to get him on his feet. He and Jeff Smith together would look like the Laurel and Hardy of the high cholesterol set.

Justin Wilson

As long as we're touring Cajun country, let's not forget Justin Wilson. Justin (he pronounces it Joos' tin) is a former down-home humorist—Jerry Clower with a dash of cayenne pepper. Now he has his own television schtick, an outdoor cooking show where he sips wine, measures everything in the palm of his hand (if at all), and detours intermittently to tell a Cajunized anecdote that most of us have heard elsewhere in a different context. The overworked Cajun mispronunciations get to be a bit much after twenty minutes or so, but his signature line ("I gay-ron-tee!") is a connecting thread that covers the show like a crazy quilt. Some days you're ready to scream if he says it one more time. Resign yourself. He will.

Justin's a genuine personality, though, and as good a good ol' boy as ever poled a pirogue down the bayou. Son-of-a-gun, he has big fun. His show's done before a live audience, which he manages to make chuckle about once a minute. He's too affable to be angry with, and nobody relishes his own cooking more than Justin.

He ends each show by eating whatever he's cooked, accompanied by much licking of chops, cries of "Who-o-o-o-o-ee!" and large quantities of wine or beer. The credits at the end don't acknowledge a designated driver to cart him away, but they should. I keep wondering if he'll ever invite members of the audience to share what he's cooked (or sipped) on camera, but I haven't seen him do it yet. Not even when he deep-fried an entire turkey in a cauldron the size of a Volkswagen.

Julia Child

Julia Child is godmother to a whole generation of cooks. The name "Julia" is as synonymous with cooking as Garlits' is with drag racing, Palmer's with golf, or Trump's with greed. Bluffers of either sex can appreciate her warm, informal approach to cooking.

Julia has written a whole shelf full of cookbooks, and her long-running television career, which began in 1963 with "The French Chef," won several Emmy awards. Today's generation can enjoy and learn from her video cassettes. Julia contends that it takes ten years to become a true chef. Her book *The Way to Cook* will set you back $50, a sum which might depress you—if you hadn't had the good sense to invest first in this bluffer's guide.

Julia, like Jeff Smith, makes cooking seem like fun. She'll breeze over her mistakes, often swearing the audience to secrecy and assuring them that *no*body'll notice if they don't tell. This culinary dynamo sweeps so many scraps onto the floor that viewers imagine the crew cleaning up afterward with a front-end loader, but it's all in the spirit of good fun and good food. If you say you prepared a main course or a dessert a certain way "because Julia said so," you gain instant respect and credibility.

Craig Claiborne

What possesses a guy to use his best silver and crystal at breakfast—and when dining alone, yet? That's the nature of dapper, flamboyant Craig Claiborne. A bachelor in his late 60s, he grew up in Mississippi, was stationed in Casablanca in the Navy during WW II, and studied cooking at the Professional School of the Swiss Hotel Keepers Association. He joined the *New York Times* as the food news editor in 1957 and finally retired in April, 1988. During his years with the *Times*, he wrote a library of some nineteen books on food and cooking, and, for twenty-five years, his annual New Year's Eve buffet for one hundred people at his home in East Hampton, New York, was such a stellar event that many people would have killed to be invited to it.

Many bluffers (and true gourmets) are aghast at the quantities of salt, sugar, fat, and cholesterol that they see going into these gurus' recipes. Some dishes would raise the cholesterol levels of innocent bystanders by 50 points. Claiborne, however, acknowledges this problem in more than one of his cookbooks, and he's even been heard to utter the C-word in public (although not too often). He deserves credit for proving that gourmet cooking can be both delicious and healthy, which to some trenchermen seems to be a contradiction in terms. If any of your guests complain that gourmet recipes use too much butter, sugar, or animal fats, you can always brandish a copy of *Craig Claiborne's Gourmet Diet* to shut them up. Or stuff an artichoke in their mouths.

James Beard

If Julia Child is the godmother of cooking, then James Beard is surely the godfather. He passed away several years ago after leaving his mark on the culinary arts for more than half a century. His work as consultant to food companies, restaurants, and homemakers rightfully earned him the title "Dean of Gastronomy."

Beard wrote cookbooks covering such areas as casseroles, breadmaking, dinner parties, barbecuing, fowl and game, and fish, but perhaps the best one for bluffers to start with is his plain and simple *The James Beard Cookbook*, which is still in print today. This book opens with practical do's and don'ts and moves on to basic equipment, weights and measures, cooking terms, and various other subjects before you even get to the recipes. The first sentence of the foreword says it all: "This is a basic cookbook." It even gives a recipe for hard-boiling eggs. Can you get much more basic than that? My copy, which I bought for a cover price of seventy-five cents when I moved into an off-campus apartment as a Florida State University junior, has survived the ensuing decades in better shape than I. It holds a sentimental place of honor in our kitchen.

A GOURMET'S GLOSSARY

Every special avocation has its own vocabulary, and gourmet cooking is no exception. Therefore, you must digest (groan) the language of the kitchen and of the assorted activities therein. Here are a few of the more common cooking terms.

Aged Steak—Beef that was forgotten in your refrigerator until it grew a coat of hairy, green mold.

Al Dente—An Italian term for food that's only half-cooked. Applied to pasta and vegetables. Not to be confused with the name of the Sicilian gentleman who operates the auto body shop and personal loan company next door to the local cement plant.

Au Jus—Served with the natural pan juices. The Americanized pronunciation is spoken as a prefatory remark while serving oneself in a family-style barbecue joint. ("Au jus' hep m'sef to this li'l sparerib rat cheer.")

Bait—See **Sushi**.

Barbeque—To roast slowly over an open fire or direct heat.

Bard—To wrap meat with bacon and tie securely before baking. Also, a poet.

Blanch—To cook briefly in boiling water. Also, to turn

suddenly pale, as when you see the overheated oil on the stove burst into flames.

Blanche—The name of the maid who cleans up the mess in the kitchen the next morning.

Bob—The name of your Golden Retriever, who probably licked the dishes clean before Blanche arrived.

Bouquet Garni—A fragrant mixture of herbs tied together in a rag and used to flavor soups and stews. Regular folks just call it an herb bag. Even an analytical chemist can't determine its contents after several hours of simmering, so you can claim *anything* is in it and no one will be the wiser. If you don't have the time to assemble one, use your cat's old catnip mouse. Nobody will know the difference by dinnertime.

Broil—To cook under heat from above. Also applies to lying in the sun too long.

Dredge—To dust with flour. Also, to retrieve a lost item from the bottom of your garbage disposal.

Mountain Oysters—The body parts that distinguish a bull from a steer. Ask your butcher to slice them and watch *him* blanch.

Poach—To cook gently in hot water. Also, to obtain meat for your main course from another's property without permission.

Reduce—To evaporate by boiling until a rich, concentrated mixture remains. Also, to shed excess pounds gained from eating your own cooking.

Render—To heat until the fat melts and drains away.

Sauté–To cook rapidly in a small amount of oil.

Sushi–Japanese term for raw fish. If you can't find it in a seafood market, try the nearest bait and tackle shop.

Sear–To cook raw meat quickly over a high flame to seal in the juices. Surgeons call it cauterizing.

COOKING WITH WINE

Wine is one of the most universal and safest ingredients to improvise with. Used in moderation, it improves the personalities of both your guests *and* your recipes. Unfortunately, the alcohol evaporates during cooking, leaving only the flavor behind.

If you're making meat stews or roasts, cheap wine works fine. Try the Chateau La Skullbuster. Some months are better vintages than others, and the best-aged bottles can be found at the back of the shelf at your nearby 7-Eleven. It has an aggressive, mischievous bouquet that caresses your tongue with all the subtlety of a sledgehammer.

As your reputation builds, you might decide to brew up some homemade wine for both drinking and cooking. Check first for symptoms of athlete's foot before you stomp the grapes, though, and hold each bottle of the finished product up to the light to examine it for clarity, color, and a stray Dr. Scholl's corn pad that may have slipped through the filtering process. Whether off-the-shelf or homemade, it's fun to keep a jug of wine handy in the kitchen whenever you're cooking. Take a slug to cleanse your palate before you taste the food. Many cooks prefer to taste their food often while it's cooking—say about every ten minutes or so—just to be sure things are coming along all right. You bet.

THE BLUFFER'S
SURVIVAL KIT

Any risky venture needs a fallback plan in case things don't work out. In gourmet cooking, this means a small shelf of life-saving products that can bail you out in case a recipe backfires and you end up with some godawful witch's brew that's only good for removing floor wax. The following items will be especially comforting to have on hand, but hide them in the garage so your guests don't find you out.

Bisquick—This stuff's been around for more than half a century, and rightly so. It's predictable, convenient, and virtually idiot-proof. Use it to make such things as coffee cakes, pancakes, pizza dough, shortcake, cookies, cobblers, muffins, and French bread. An early slogan called it "A world of baking in a box." All you have to do is follow directions to turn out a whole array of baked goods that you can claim you made "from scratch." The manufacturer, General Mills, recently introduced a cholesterol-free version with no animal fats or tropical oils, and the baking results are as reliable as they were in 1931.

Instant mashed potatoes—Use to thicken anything from gravy to wallpaper paste.

Ready-made spaghetti sauce—Add a little of your own oregano, garlic, and rosemary to change the prefab flavor, then claim it's your own secret recipe. What's secret, of course, is what you did to it after it came out of the jar.

Assorted prepackaged mixes—Your nearby supermarket will have an enormous rack of these that'll boggle the mind. Everything from chili and taco to foreign and uptown sauces and salad dressings. Add a little water, oil, milk, or whatever, and you've got something that would have taken ten times longer if you'd have had to assemble all the ingredients yourself. Assuming, of course, you knew how in the first place. And since you're a bluffer, you don't.

Beef and chicken bouillon cubes—These are good substitutes for beef or chicken stock. The alternative is to simmer beef or chicken scraps in a large kettle or stock pot for a day or two, reducing the liquid to a rich broth. Either way, the end result's about the same. The only hassle you'll get with a bouillon cube is trying to get the darned thing to dissolve, but it sure beats wrestling a five-gallon stock pot all over the kitchen (and refrigerating it overnight).

Food coloring—A lifesaver when whatever it is that you're cooking suddenly turns puce or taupe or chartreuse for no apparent reason. Buy assorted colors, but be sure to get a jumbo bottle of green; you'll use it a lot on St. Patrick's Day.

Various microwave dinners—Use your own judgment here. A good supply of nuke-a-meals can go a long way toward relieving your dinner party jitters. Hide them in the back of the freezer so nobody sees them. If you're forced to fall back on them in a crisis and worry that the microwave beeper will blow your cover, ask a qualified technician to disconnect it.

Campbell's soup – Several companies have gone up against Campbell's in the canned soup market and been handed their heads – or worse. Campbell's market share is rock-solid, just like venerable Bisquick's. The company seems to introduce a new flavor about every other week, so you've got plenty to choose from. As far as bluffers are concerned, Campbell's slogan "Soup is good food" could be rephrased "Soup is good insurance." Against mistakes, that is. Campbell's soup is every bit as user-friendly as Bisquick. Just follow the directions.

A friend who's a maitre d' at a local restaurant – Save this ace in the hole for an outright emergency. You can call him for advice if anything goes wrong (he can ask the chef – if the chef's in a decent mood, which few of them are). If your venture into the gourmet cooking arena turns out to be a *total* catastrophe, you can always laugh to keep from crying and ask your maitre d' pal to make reservations for dinner.

Visa, MasterCard, or American Express – To charge dinner for your guests at the above restaurant.

KITCHEN DECOR

People will jump to all kinds of conclusions about your culinary ability based on how your kitchen looks. Give them a little nudge or two by making it a showcase for your talent—or what passes for such.

Miscellaneous Equipment

Display several of your most expensive and foreign-made small appliances and gadgets in plain sight. These should definitely include your pasta machine, spice grinder, food processor, and KitchenAid mixer, along with several of its more intriguing attachments (dough hook, sausage grinder, hedge trimmer, paper shredder, etc.). Line them up like good soldiers in your war on ho-hum dining.

Dried Herbs, etc.

Hang the aforementioned strings of dried chilies or garlic swags where they're sure to be noticed by anyone who walks in the kitchen. Supplement these by hanging small bunches of dried herbs upside down throughout the room. Claim they're from your herb garden, if you have one. Within a few days their aromas will blend to give your kitchen the atmosphere of a true gourmet's grotto.

Seasonings Rack

People often assume that the fisherman with the biggest tackle box is the most savvy of all. The same concept applies to cooks. The larger the rack of seasonings hanging on your wall, the greater your prowess as a gourmet cook. Theoretically, that is.

Since people conclude a lot about your ability from your array of herbs and spices, buy the largest rack you can find (or have it custom made) and hang it in plain sight. Then stock it with prestige brands, such as Spice Islands (never Watkins), and include a generous number of strange items, such as turmeric, whole nutmeg, arrowroot, and mace.

You don't necessarily have to use the expensive stuff in your cooking, of course. If you're on a budget, buy bargain-basement brands, perhaps some private label from a discount supermarket chain, and hide them in a drawer for everyday use. Leave your expensive brands for display purposes only. An alternative would be to go ahead and use the expensive stuff and restock the jars with a cheaper brand when your supply runs low. After all, one bay leaf looks about the same as another, right? If you're careful not to scuff or tear the labels, the jars should last for years without anyone catching on.

Overhead Cookware Rack

This is one of those oval-shaped, metal, Spanish-looking contraptions that's usually suspended from the ceiling on heavy chains. It has hooks running all around the side. Look for them in the kitchenware department of expensive department stores, on television cooking shows, and in restaurant kitchens. They're a great way to display your cookware, and if you *really* want to go first class and buy lots of copper pots and pans, they deserve to swing from one of these (watch your head though). When you're not entertaining, use the hooks to hang up drip-dry laundry, neckties, belts, and small, hyperactive children.

THINGS TO BE
FUSSY ABOUT

People assume that all great chefs are temperamental, so bluffers have every right be a little quirky. There's a lot of tradition and image at stake here. You can find plenty of things to be fussy about, so what follows are only a few suggestions.

Stirring Properly

There's more to stirring food than clanking a spoon around the sides of a pot. In fact, that's no way to stir much of anything, even cement. The end result, if you keep it up long enough, is about the same as if you'd run the stuff through a food processor.

Insist on stirring in opposing figure-8 patterns, which tend to cover the bottom of the pan well and keep food from sticking and burning. If you're a vintage aircraft buff, stir in the pattern of a WW II P-51 Mustang 4-bladed prop. Scrape the sides of the pan occasionally, because what slops up on them will eventually dry and harden. If it flakes off and drops back down into the pan, it'll make the food taste bad. On second thought, in your case, it might improve the flavor.

What happens if you cook something too long and it ends up soldered to the bottom of the pan? Well, all's not necessarily lost. Depending on the ingredients, maybe you can add equal parts of flour and fat and stir until it turns some shade of brown. Cajun cooks do this on purpose. They call it roux.

If you're mixing fragile ingredients, such as avocados and diced tomatoes, fold them together with a lift-and-turn motion to keep from grinding them into anonymity and ending up with some revolting mystery mess to be served amid much gagging and choruses of "What's *that?*"

If guests wander into the kitchen and start lifting the lids of your pots and pans and tasting while you're doing serious stirring, this is an excellent opportunity to conduct a short seminar on Proper Stirring. After you've grabbed the spoon defensively and threatened them with a rolling pin, demonstrate the proper way to stir while injecting remarks like "It's all in the wrist" or "This is the *proper* way to do it, according to Julia (or Craig, or Jeff, or Paul, or James, or even Joos' tin)."

A final point about stirring: don't *bang* the spoon on the top of the pot. This seems to be Jeff Smith's pet peeve, and his voice hits high C every time he mentions it. You'll put nicks and dents in the rim, which will make the lid fit poorly and allow steam and flavor to escape. Don't *do* it!

Cast-Iron Cookware

Funny how things come full circle. Several generations ago, cast-iron cookware was as common as dirt. Ceramic and Teflon-coated skillets and sauce pans were non-existent. Your great-grandparents had a choice between either cast iron or a flat rock. Today, cast iron's back in fashion again. Is that progress or what?

Cast-iron pots and skillets add an earthy, down-home, country-kitchen atmosphere to your kitchen, and they're almost indispensable for certain Cajun and Tex-Mex dishes, which might melt less sturdy stuff. You can get in trouble, though, if the metal isn't seasoned properly.

Manufacturers typically suggest that you rub cooking oil (peanut oil works well) into the pores of a new cast-iron utensil, both inside and out, then put it into a 300-degree oven for an hour or so. This treatment prevents the outside from rusting and keeps the inside from burning and sticking. After the initial seasoning, follow the rule of "hot skillet, cold oil." That is, heat the surface until water dances around on it, *then* add the oil. After several uses, you'll notice that the cooking surface takes on a black, smooth patina and you can cook with a minimum amount of oil.

A well-seasoned set of cast-iron cookware is a gourmet's pride and joy. It should be washed with mild liquid dish detergent and hot water and immediately wiped dry. Never, *never* use scouring pads or cleansers. Properly cared for, cast-iron cookware won't rust and should last forever. And if you catch any Harry or Harriet Helpful scrubbing away in your carefully nurtured Number 12 cast-iron skillet with Ajax, you should gently tell them to stop. Then carve a standing rib roast out of them with a chain saw.

Sequence of Mixing Ingredients

This is fair game for any bluffer to be peculiar about.

You can claim (and who can refute it?) that certain ingredients must be added in a specific order; otherwise, the entire character of the recipe changes. Such is true of everything from a decorated nut bombe to the detonation of a neutron bomb. It's the old domino theory. Each part of a recipe is affected by the procedures and additions that preceded it and those that will follow. Line up the ingredients and seasonings in precise order, like a magician with his props, and start down the line, adding and stirring and timing the introduction of each one into the pot with meticulous precision and great fanfare.

As you add ingredients, mutter concern about the flavors being "married" properly. This attention to properly sanctioned culinary matrimony implies that you're determined to extract maximum flavor and contribution from each and every ingredient. You're talking long-term commitment here, not just a one-night stand.

Certain Utensils for Certain Dishes

Use your imagination. You can declare one certain skillet Off Limits for everything but omelets, reserve another one exclusively for blackened fish, and use one pot (preferably cast iron) specifically for chili. Attach little labels that say "FOR _____ ONLY!" to impress your guests and further your image as a true purist. Mumble "flavor contamination" or "uncomplementary seasonings" if you're challenged. Carry the idea too far, though, and you're going to run out of space in your kitchen, and you'll have to branch out to another storage area. Like the garage.

Fresh vs. Dried Ingredients

If there's a gourmet shop within commuting distance, you'll probably be able to stock various seasonings in their natural, fresh-cut state. Others may be preferred dried, or may be so nearly inaccessible that they're hard to find any way other than dried. Then hold forth about *specific* herbs and spices. Be emphatic about which ones *must* be fresh.

An herb garden, as mentioned earlier, helps resolve your dilemma about finding some rare, hard-to-find items. Just grow your own–as long as they're not controlled substances commonly rolled up and smoked. You can buy seeds by mail if they aren't available locally. Check the appendixes of several cookbooks for the addresses of suppliers.

When cooking with dried seasonings, you can project an instant gourmet image by mixing them together in a bowl and setting it out *before* your guests arrive. This admittedly conflicts with your being fanatical about the sequence of mixing some things, but you'll have to reconcile the two images. This way, however, you don't have to do anything fancy; just use whatever seasonings the recipe calls for. Just make sure they're colorful and of different textures. Your local aquarium store can offer a variety of tropical fish foods which would serve quite nicely. What happens when people see this concoction on your counter? Instant awe.

"What's *this?*"

"Oh, er, just a little blend of my own."

"It smells . . . terrific!"

"Yeah, well, I put seven . . . no, *nine* different things in it."

"Like what?"

(Smiling mysteriously, you can now select from a variety of answers.)

• "That's *my* little secret."

• "It was whispered to me by a certified executive chef on his *death*bed."

• ".Sorry, my lawyer told me not to disclose the ingredients to anyone – not even to my mother – until General Mills raises their offer to at *least* half a million dollars."

• "Be patient. It'll be for sale in *every* supermarket and gourmet shop in the country in a month or two."

• "If I told you, you'd *never* believe me."

Adjusting Seasonings

Cooks should taste their dishes while cooking to be sure the seasonings are in correct proportion. As far as you're concerned, they'll always have to be adjusted because the process gives you the perfect opportunity to impress your friends.

First, make a big display of tasting the food. Take a modest sample, then close your eyes. Rotate your tongue clockwise or counterclockwise in your mouth (either direction is acceptable, although classically trained chefs seem to prefer the latter). Smack your lips slightly and murmur under your breath as if your tastebuds are giving you an instant analysis and digital readout of whatever it is you're tasting.

Feel free to repeat the above process at least once, then go about adjusting the seasonings. Add a pinch of this and a dash of that, stir it carefully (see previous discussion), taste it again, and nod your head judiciously. The miniscule amount of seasonings that you added couldn't possibly make any difference in the flavor of the entire kettle, but if you're a good actor, your guests will believe that *you* can tell the difference. Therein lies your mystique.

Do make sure to use the word "adjust" when describing this activity to your guests. "Adjust" reeks with professionalism. You'd sound like a clod if you say, "Well, I've gotta go check how this stuff tastes now," and then plow into the task. Surgeons don't do surgery; they "perform" it. Cops don't haul someone off to jail; they "take them into custody." Lawyers aren't just hired guns who can manipulate the legal system; they're "attorneys and counselors at law." So, as a bluffer-gourmet, will you merely "add to" or "check" your seasonings? Hell, no. You'll "adjust" them, okay?

Measuring in Liters

Measuring in liters gives you a certain Continental flair. In addition, your guests have more trouble figuring out that you don't know what you're doing. If you can't convert to metric measurements, don't worry. Just look around on the other side of your Pyrex measuring cup and bingo! It's calibrated in ounces. Some of the most perplexing problems have absurdly simple answers.

COOKING WITH FLAIR

Anybody can follow a recipe and sling hash on a plate. Bluffer gourmets, like geisha girls, appreciate one universal truth: a touch of flair can add a lot of pizazz to an otherwise mundane mechanical experience. Showmanship makes the difference.

Experience will provide plenty of ways to jazz up your cooking and serving performance, but here are several things to start out with.

Knife-Juggling

Ever have dinner at a Japanese steak house? If so, you can really appreciate the show. Japanese chefs are masters at flippin' steel. They're probably descendants of itinerant knife-jugglers who performed in turn-of-the-century sideshows in traveling carnivals. Using his fingernails alone, a good Japanese chef can butterfly a dozen shrimp before you can say "banzai!"

Don't try too much fancy knife-juggling, though, until you've practiced. A lot. And alone. Try it first with table knives (like some guests, they're comfortably dull) and advance to the sharper-edged variety as you build experience, confidence, and courage.

When you get proficient enough to try your skill in front of guests, have at it. First, however, make sure, that your homeowners liability insurance is paid up in case you miss catching a tumbling, razor-sharp knife, and the wife of one of your guests – who just happens to be a personal injury lawyer – gets an impromptu nose job or a discount face lift. Just don't be surprised if you're hauled into court for practicing surgery without a license.

Mixing and Serving Drinks

Lots of folks are amazed by the sleight-of-hand performances of flamboyant bartenders. They flip beer bottles end over end, uncap them with a crash-and-smash motion against the edge of the bar, and slam both the foaming bottle and a glass down in front of the astonished customer before you can say "Spuds MacKenzie" or "Call an ambulance."

You'll probably find the best example of this alcoholic derring-do in the movie *Cocktail,* starring Tom Cruise. Rent a videotape; you'll see what I mean. It's a heck of a lot cheaper than paying $3 a drink to see a live performance, assuming there's a bar in your town that really allows bartenders to *do* that crazy stuff. If you thought juggling knives was risky, check out these guys. One slip, and it's concussion city.

You can waste plenty of good booze practicing alcoholic acrobatics, so use bottles of water first. Keep a mop, broom, and dustpan handy to clean up the water and broken glass. Don't practice in your bare feet. Wear a motorcycle helmet. Remove the shards of glass embedded in the walls and ceiling before your guests arrive.

When you're ready to go for the big time, ask a bartender buddy for some empty liquor bottles with expensive labels. Pour some rotgut inside, so if you

miss a toss and suffer a loss, it's no big deal. And if your show comes off without a hitch, your guests will be so spellbound with your showmanship that they probably won't notice how awful your drinks taste. The same principle of benign deception was suggested, you'll recall, in stocking your spice rack. The bottles should last indefinitely if you don't scuff the labels. One of my fraternity brothers in college, "Frugal Fred" O'Malley, was a legend in his time. He got three semesters' service out of the same Seagram's Crown Royal bottle. His dates never knew the difference, and they surely were impressed. ("Wow! *Crown Royal?*" "Of course, baby! Nothin' but the best for you!") "Frugal Fred" is now a successful trash recycling consultant to large municipalities.

Wardrobe and Accessories

"Looking the part," said captain of industry Malcolm Forbes, "helps get the chance to fill it." The same logic applies to bluffers in gourmet cooking. If you look like a cook, guests will assume you are. Silly them.

Tops on your list should be a chef's tunic. It looks extremely Continental and infinitely more professional than a red and white checkered apron emblazoned with a cornball remark like "Hail to the chef" or "For this I spent four years in college?" Shop for a tunic with a fancy coat of arms on the pocket, or buy a plain one and find some kind of official-looking insignia, perhaps cut from a blazer at a Salvation Army Thrift Shop, and sew it on yourself. Then claim (with aw-shucks, downcast eyes and modestly fluttering eyelashes) that the tunic is a memento from your years of service as an executive chef at "a charming little 4-star restaurant in Paris." Paris, Texas, that is.

And no chef is really cookin' (moan, groan) without one of those tall, pleated, funny-looking white hats. They have all the practicality of the powdered Shirley Temple wigs that English magistrates wear. All right, so they look weird (that's putting it charitably), but they're part of your tonsorial package. Can you imagine Tammy Faye Bakker without mascara or an avuncular Chairman of the Board without a necktie? Enough said.

Then there's the matter of shoes. You have a choice here between a traditional white, low-cut style with cushioned rubber soles or high-top sneakers. Go with the sneakers. They've got built-in arch supports (for those bone-jarring slam dunks into the kitchen waste-basket), and they absorb spills. After you've dripped enough sauces and seasonings onto them, you can simmer them overnight in a large kettle. The result? An intriguing soup that *nobody* will be able to guess the contents of, much less duplicate. Then run the sneakers through the washing machine with a little bleach and detergent, and they're ready to go again!

Now let's talk accessories. First, get yourself a set of measuring spoons – metal ones – and wear them on a cord attached to your belt. They make a wonderful racket as they clang and bang while you hustle and bustle to and fro in the kitchen. Their obvious purpose is to be at the ready in case you have to measure some critical ingredient in a hurry and don't want to hunt around to find them. Their real purpose, however, is to impress your guests with the sound of all the frenetic activity going on in the kitchen.

You'll also look extra sharp and professional if you

attach a wiping rag to your belt. This comes in handy for cleaning splattered gravy off the rims of plates, wiping your fingers, and mopping up unsightly spills from your kitchen floor.

Exotically Colored Pastas

Pasta is an especially good menu item because it's really hard to screw up. I mean, all you have to do is put it into boiling water and set the timer.

Breaking with tradition, several companies now make pasta out of spinach. It's a medium shade of green, and when served with a tomato sauce, it adds a rich, festive flair to your Christmas table. The taste is nearly the same as traditional pasta, which makes this an odds-on favorite with mothers. They can get their kids to eat vegetables and not even realize it. Life's other challenges should be so easy.

You can certainly improvise far beyond the humble limits of store-bought spinach pasta, though. Use regular pasta and a little food coloring to produce lots of "theme" dinners; heck, you can even cook several different colors and mix them together for a technicolor effect. Consider these "colorful" occasions:

Kelly green	St. Patrick's Day
Black	Anniversary of the '29 stock market crash
Red	The day your mortgage payment's due
Blue	When you break up with your current pelvic affiliate

Camouflage (green, black, tan, and brown)	Late-night dinners after watching the latest *Rambo* flick
Red, white, and blue	Fourth of July
Every color of the rainbow	Your next far-out, groovy, psychedelic Woodstock memorial reunion

Helpful hint: add a little oil to the cooking water to keep the pasta from sticking together like a ball of Elmer's glue after you drain and rinse it.

ETHNIC AND REGIONAL DISHES, OR INDIGESTION GOES INTERNATIONAL

Bluffers need to display at least a working knowledge of various ethnic and regional dishes. Here, for your discriminating approval, are several suggestions, along with some key points to remember and a few popular ingredients used in each dish.

Italian

Nobody but *nobody* charges headlong into cooking and eating with the gusto that Italians do. They're more basic and earthy than the French and don't befoul their cuisine with strange, obscure things like fungi (truffles) and snails (escargot). It's said that Neapolitan cooks fling a piece of pasta against the wall to test for doneness. If it sticks there for a count of three, it's ready. We're talkin' regular folks here!

Main points to remember Put a tablespoon or two of oil in the water before cooking pasta so it won't stick together (mentioned previously). Also rinse the drained pasta with clean, boiling water to wash away much of the starch that has boiled out in the cooking water. Save the cooking water if you like starch in your shirts.

Keep several wicker-encased bottles of Chianti sitting around your kitchen. At least one should have a candle stuck in the top and lots of colored wax cascading down the neck. (You can buy special multicolored dripping candles that will do this in a few hours instead of spending five years to get the same effect.)

Avoid using the word "authentic" in connection with pizza, which is more American than Italian. You might mention, though, that the pizza's godfather (pun intended) was the rugged flat loaves of bread that Roman legions ate as they trekked off to scare the hell out of much of the world. Historians compare this bread to the shape of a modern Frisbee, and it was almost as indestructible.

Some popular ingredients Italians love sweet green peppers fixed just about any way, but roasted sweet red peppers in garlic and olive oil are an adventure to contemplate and a revelation to experience. There's also nothing quite as savory as link sausage made with traditional Italian herbs and spices. Some of the more popular seasonings are fennel, rosemary, garlic, fresh plum tomatoes, tomato sauce and paste, and olive oil. Oregano, which seems to be used in just about everything, is a patently Italian seasoning. Sometimes called "the pizza herb," its scent and flavor put an indelible Italian signature on any recipe.

French

The French would like the rest of us to believe that they invented cooking, and who's to say they didn't? French dishes have an unassailable mystique, and the reputation of many French restaurants is legendary.

Main points to remember Act snobbish and arrogant whenever you prepare French food. Your guests won't mind; in fact, they'll probably expect it. If you can fake an accent successfully, that's even better. Check out some old Maurice Chevalier movies on late-night television.

It's generally a good idea to insist on using fresh ingredients (with the exception of certain herbs and spices), but the French have a special obsession with freshness. You too can make a big point of this, of course, by leaving vegetables and other ingredients on your counter in the paper bags they came home in from the farmer's market. Or lay them out and claim that you just brought them in from the back yard.

The French love crescent rolls, which they call "croissants." To get the correct pronunciation, pinch your nostrils closed with two fingers and say "craw-saw." Cheese, like croissants, is universally popular and comes in an enormous array of flavors and textures.

Last but not least, the French are obsessed with sauces. All kinds of sauces. Check 'em out.

Some popular ingredients Truffles (fungi) and escargot (snails) are considered synonymous with French cooking. Truffles go for a modest $200 per pound, and they're rooted out of the forest floor by the snouts of trained pigs. Now, is that class or what? Some cooks have declared them (the truffles, not the pigs) pretentious and optional, and the price may soon decline because American versions are now being cultivated. Coming soon to a moldy, wooded glen near you. Wine is an indispensable ingredient that improves the flavor of many recipes. Use it liberally because in your case you'll probably need all the help you can get.

The French also use lots of parsley and herbs, such as thyme, basil, chervil, and tarragon, which grow wild in many places. I've even seen a recipe for nasturtium soup. Rumor has it that in France you'll soon be able to send a bowl to friends by an FTD florist.

You're on safe ground if you use plenty of mushrooms (a relative of the truffle). Bouillabaisse is an especially colorful and adventuresome main course if you're having a large party and want to serve assorted seafood that's all cooked together in the same pot.

Spanish

Although this cuisine shares many ingredients and flavors with other countries, Spanish cooking retains a character all its own. Many of the best Spanish recipes are seafood dishes, and the Spanish onion is a mainstay of multinational recipes.

Main points to remember Flan, a type of custard, is virtually the national dessert. The Spanish, like the Italians and the French, are very big on wine – both for cooking and for drinking. Insist on fresh instead of frozen ingredients, of course.

Some popular ingredients Saffron, olive oil, pork, assorted seafood (notably clams, scallops, hake, and even eels and octopus), hot and mild peppers, paprika, tomatoes, onions, chorizos (spicy Spanish sausages), and various dried beans, especially garbanzo and black beans. Almonds are also very popular.

Chinese

The Chinese are noted for simple recipes that use

a miniscule amount of meat and generous amounts of vegetables which, when combined with some of their other ingredients, yield a flavor that's patently unique. A Chinese-Russian restaurant recently opened in my city. The food was excellent, but an hour later customers complained that they were hungry for power.

China will be forever remembered for giving us the wok, which is perhaps the most simple and versatile cooking utensil ever invented.

Main points to remember Classic woks are made of cast iron, which means you have to season and treat them like you would any other cast-iron cookware. If you're not a purist, you can buy a Teflon-coated electric model that can be used in the middle of the table. Lots of recipes are either stir-fried or deep-fried, which makes a wok an indispensable utensil for cooking just about anything Chinese. A bamboo steamer is also a must-have item, because many vegetables are served either steamed or mildly annoyed.

Climatic conditions prevent various Chinese ingredients from being readily available in this country, so don't commit yourself to serving a particular dish before you're sure you can get all the sauce and dried items that it calls for. Keep several Chun King heat 'n eat dinners on hand in case one of your made-from-scratch recipes backfires.

Some popular ingredients Assorted vegetables (including bamboo shoots, water chestnuts, snow peas, and scallions), rice wine, chow mein noodles, soy sauce, hot peppers, pork, sugar, sesame seed oil, ginger (freshly chopped), dried black mushrooms, and – of course – rice. Sambal olek, a fiery red chinese chili pepper sauce, is hot. Go easy. It could start a nuclear meltdown. In fact, it's so lethal that it should be sold in child-proof containers.

Cajun

Cajun cooking was born in the Louisiana bayou country, and lots of us give thanks for that blessed event. It's one of America's most distinctive regional cuisines.

Although Paul Prudhomme's cookbook is acknowledged as one of the finest, you can't go wrong by picking up one of a host of Cajun/Creole cookbooks that are published as fundraising projects by various Louisiana women's service leagues. One that comes to mind is the *Shadows-on-the-Teche Cookbook,* published by the Shadows Service League of New Iberia, Louisiana. It's got bayou country recipes from decades before the Civil War. Such books are a charming blend of history and authenticity that complement any bluffer-gourmet's library.

Main points to remember "Cajun," you can state authoritatively, "is an aberration of *Acadian."* The Acadians were French who settled in Nova Scotia in the 1600s in a colony they called Acadia. The British ran them out of Nova Scotia around 1750, and a goodly number headed for Louisiana, where previous French settlers welcomed them and absorbed them into the ways of bayou country living, which meant living off the land by fishing, farming, and trapping.

Cajun cooking is a rowdy celebration of flavors — gumbos, jambalayas, étouffées, and a mystical blend of seasonings that have something to teach even the most educated palate. Its history is essentially French, but with more gusto and less arrogance. Although it shares ingredients and seasonings with Creole cooking, Paul Prudhomme declares that Creole cooking is an amalgamation of French, Italian, African, Spanish, American Indian, and other ethnic groups that settled around New Orleans. Cajun cooking, he maintains, is a less sophisticated, more down-home type of cooking, but the distinction, for all intents and purposes, is becoming more and more esoteric.

Some popular ingredients Rice, pork, assorted seafoods, cayenne pepper, garlic, paprika, Tabasco sauce, okra, filé powder, red onions, red beans, black-eyed peas, okra, and any other vegetables you can lay your hands on. Zatarain's crab boil, which is made in Louisiana, is a blend of what looks to be several dozen seasonings in a plastic bag. If you lean over the boiling kettle and take a deep breath, it'll clear your sinuses in a heartbeat. Use it for cooking shrimp, crabs, and crawfish.

Tex-Mex

Tex-Mex cooking is a bulging collection of down-home, rough-and-rugged simple recipes that have sustained generations of leathery old ranchers and cowpokes since frontier times. Like Cajun and Creole cooking, it's rooted in American history. Tex-Mex food is reminiscent of iron kettles over campfires, sourdough bread, tumbleweeds, ten-gallon hats, faded Levi's, saddle sores, and sweaty men wearing unlicensed firearms gathered around a chuckwagon after bedding the herd down for the night. Yippie-I-O-K-i-A-y.

Main points to remember Chili, tacos, burritos,

salsa, and creative variations thereof form the foundation of Tex-Mex cooking. The traditional chili cook-off that's been unique to Texas for generations has now spread to other parts of the country. Nothing compares with listening to a bunch of salty old chiliheads in authentic western garb arguing the merits of various ingredients and cooking techniques while squatting around an open campfire – in New Jersey.

Chili is an art form. Because no two chiliheads agree on what the "best" chili is, feel free to declare yourself an "expert." Everyone else is. Some eccentric chili cookoff participants have used such strange ingredients as possum, armadillo, and (I am not kidding) a handful of dirt. The battle rages about whether "real" chili should be made with beans or not, and whether the meat should be cut up in 1" chunks (half beef, half pork) or ground up like hamburger. Some self-proclaimed experts swear that chili isn't chili unless it's made in a cast-iron pot over an open fire, but this could pose some problems if you're living in a fifth-floor condo.

The flavor of chili usually improves if you allow it to age for at least 24 hours. Don't be tempted to dispose of that "lid" of grease.

Some popular ingredients Chili powder, green and red chili peppers, avocados, onions, tomatoes, tomato sauce, jalapeno peppers, cumin, Monterey Jack cheese, Alka Seltzer (taken separately as a nightcap), and plenty of beer – both for cooking and for drinking. Several brands of chili mix, including Wick Fowler's and Carroll Shelby's, make preparing a chili dinner fairly fail-safe.

Barbecue

Barbecue's origins aren't as regional as Tex-Mex cooking. In fact, you'll find "authentic" barbecue joints strung from Virginia to California. If you're a barbecue fan, imagine the dedication of Greg Johnson and Vince Staten, two guys who drove some 40,000 miles and visited more than 700 barbecue joints while gathering material for their book *Real BBQ,* which was published in 1988. Such self-sacrifice in the pursuit of knowledge, combined with fumes from superheated versions of secret barbecue sauce, brings tears to the eyes of even dedicated barbecue freaks.

I was once a regular customer in a barbecue joint in South Hill, Virginia, that slow cooked pork shoulders in four or five stages above an open fire. They started on the top rack and moved down one level each day until they were about a foot above the hickory fire, and then they were done. The owner, a guy named Nate, could pull the meat off the bone with his fingers. On Friday nights, the local police department (all three officers) almost had to direct traffic in the parking lot.

Main points to remember Barbecue sauce, like chili, is always evolving. It's never perfect. This quest for the best (and "best" is one heck of a judgment call) is what makes it so darn much fun. Improvisation is the rule, not the exception. You can start with a favorite sauce recipe but vary the proportions and ingredients from one time to the next and never produce the exact same taste every time. That, along with keeping your recipe a sworn secret, is part of barbecue's charm.

Barbecue sauce is about as regional as dialects. Some parts of the country (or even a state) prefer tomato-based sauce; others, mustard-based. Some like it thin and vinegary, while others opt for a consistency somewhere between house paint and oatmeal that you slather on the meat with a paint brush or a mop.

Sometimes barbecue addicts get so preoccupied with debating the virtues of their secret sauce recipes that the meat itself becomes an afterthought. The idea, though, is to cook it s-l-o-w-l-y—so it falls apart. If you use a charcoal fire, periodically throw on a handful of wood chips soaked in water to give the meat a genuine wood-smoked flavor and a reddish coloring that penetrates beneath the surface. Hickory chips are the traditional and a very flavorful choice, although mesquite has become popular in recent years.

Don't baste the meat with tomato-based barbecue sauce throughout the cooking process. Bad mistake. It'll end up with a charred coating that looks and tastes like epoxy. The right way to use a tomato-based sauce is to rub the meat with salt, pepper, and any other seasonings first, and apply the sauce during the final 20-30 minutes of cooking—or perhaps not until serving. On the other hand, if you use a vinegar-based sauce, you can baste the meat from start to finish.

Some popular ingredients Beer (for drinking), dry mustard, onions, vinegar, tomato sauce, salad mustard, hot red pepper flakes, cayenne pepper, brown sugar, black pepper, hickory or mesquite chips or chunks.

Pork is perhaps the most popular meat, but there are plenty of beef and chicken fans out there, too. Within the past several years, places have sprung up all over the country that specialize in serving chicken wings tastefully prepared in the fine old tradition of that culinary mecca, Buffalo, New York.

English

English cooking has gotten a bad rap for years, but many English dishes taste quite good. Better, sometimes, than the food that's served on them.

Humor aside (but not for too long), you'll probably find more oddly named recipes and strange terms in English cookbooks than in most others: Toad-in-the-Hole, Bangers and Bloaters, Soused Mackerel, Bubble and Squeak, and Spotted Dick. One recipe for Jugged Hare lists the first ingredient as "One hare, well-hung." The term means drained for several hours, but it's a hoot to imagine a butcher's reaction if you really ordered one that way: "Whaddaya wanna do, cook it or make love to it?" Or picture two English gentlemen, shotguns at the ready, taking aim at a fleeing hare:

"What do you think, Nigel? Should we bring down this bloke or wait for a better one, eh wot?"

"The blighter's moving too bloody fast, Percival! I can't get a proper look!"

Main points to remember: Some English food and drink are traditional at holiday time: Plum Pudding, Yorkshire Pudding, Mulled Wine. The English supposedly created the watercress sandwich, and watercress is often substituted for lettuce in salads. It's a sharp-tasting, leafy green vegetable that resembles clover, except you have to gather it from creeks and ponds. One of the best English contributions to seasonings is Coleman's dry mustard, which is used in multinational recipes and happens to be Jeff Smith's favorite brand (a point you should emphasize whenever you can). Worcestershire sauce, of course, is famous the world over.

If you're throwing a party with an English Pub theme, be sure to say "bloke" and "mate" and "blimey" a lot. Hang a couple of dart boards in your recreation room, because darts in English pubs are as common as tweed jackets. If you're lucky enough to have a newsstand that sells foreign newspapers, throw down several copies of the *London Daily Mail* strategically throughout the room. To top things off, serve beer in genuine English Ravenhead glass pub mugs, the kind with big dimples all around the sides. You can buy them through several American mail-order catalogs. Your guests can see the logo and brand name on the bottom when they take a drink. I know. I just checked. Ravenhead mugs put the final stamp of authenticity on the claim that you're an Anglophile.

As for English beer—well, that's no problem. You can buy Watney's Red Barrel, Guinness, and Bass at any respectable supermarket that sells imported brands. In fact, with a little geographic license, you can venture north to Ireland (alcoholically speaking) to serve Harp or several other Irish brews.

Some popular ingredients: English recipes use lots of potatoes, onions, tomatoes, apples, and berries. Beef, lamb, and kidneys (as in steak and kidney pie) are popular. Horseradish is a patently English condiment when served as a complement to roast beef. Cheddar cheese is commonplace, and English muffins are now as much a part of American culture as the English language itself. Unless, of course, you happen to be from the Deep South, y'all.

German

The mere mention of Germany calls to mind spired, majestic castles along the Rhine, funny-looking low-slung dogs with stubby legs, hot, vinegary potato salad, delectable sausages, pungent sauerkraut, and incomparable cakes, pies, and pastries that'll make you gain ten pounds just by walking past the bakery window. Germany also calls to mind burly guys named Hans or Fritz wearing lederhosen and felt hats, who'll go upside your head with an alpenstock and escort you out of a German beer hall headfirst if you belch too loud while the oompah-pah band is playing. But that's another story.

Back to the subject. The Germans are world-renowned for their hearty drinking and dining, which has led many people to think of the stereotypical German as Sergeant Schultz on *Hogan's Heroes* reruns. Although some gastronomic snobs call German cooking "peasant food," its grass-roots ingredients and the ways in which they're prepared are uniquely Teutonic and terrific. Remember, this is the country that gave us Black Forest cake, Westphalian ham, and Liederkranz and Limburger cheese (phew!), not to mention a host of classical musicians, poets, authors, and high-octane beer strong enough to power Porsches to successive victories at Le Mans.

Main points to remember: When it comes to main courses, people usually think of recipes that contain sauerbraten, sausages, sauerkraut, cabbage, dumplings, and potatoes. That's okay; don't disappoint them. After all, you can cook that kind of stuff in your crock pot while you go off and spend the day celebrating life. When you get home, dinner will be ready.

If you want to come on like a rootin' tootin' Teutonic chef, though, you'll have to sharpen your prowess with making pastries, strudels, and rough, hearty breads like pumpernickel. Left to age for a week or so, a loaf of pumpernickel is great for sanding furniture and hardwood floors.

How to hone those baking skills, you may ask? Glad you asked that. Start with your fingers. Walk through the Yellow Pages of the phone book until you find the name of a good German bakery. Now, was that easy or what?

Some popular ingredients: There's nothing too fancy here. Many German recipes use regular-folks roadside-market stuff like cabbage, potatoes, pork, apples, assorted nuts, berries, fruit, cheese, caraway seeds, onions, and parsley. German recipes also use lots of wild game, such as venison and boar, which may be hard to find in your area unless you have a close friend who works the night shift at the local zoo.

Greek

Greeks, like Italians, are a hearty, festive people who love to eat and drink with gusto. They prefer to celebrate holidays by barbecuing whole four-legged creatures over open pits and singing and dancing a lot.

Some gourmets swear that no other salad can compete with an authentic Greek salad. This symphony of flavors, composed of Greek peppers, feta cheese, potatoes, assorted green and ripe olives, oregano, lettuce, tomatoes, onions, and seasoned olive oil dressing, defies description. Let's just say it's *good*. Greek restaurants serve them either as a side dish or as a main course, so you can't go wrong either way.

The Greeks also gave us gyro sandwiches, a delicious combination of thinly sliced, highly spiced lamb, cucumbers, tomatoes, lettuce, onions, and sour cream. All of this is wrapped in a soft, round piece of bread that resembles a thick tortilla. Uninitiated gyro eaters usually end up eating half the sandwich with their hands and the other half with a fork, after the filling has fallen all over their plates or (more often than not) into their laps.

Because both Greek and Turkish foods are rooted in the ancient Byzantine empire, don't be surprised if your guests mistake a Greek recipe for a Turkish one. A simple bluffer's reply might be, "It's Greek to me."

Main points to remember: Moussaka, a minced-meat pie made with beef or mutton, is very popular. Every bluffer should know about baklava (pronounced bock'-law-vaw), a rich, sweet Greek pastry dessert served in small, diamond-shaped pieces. One taste and you'll be hooked.

Since Greeks like to celebrate just about everything, holidays are great times to serve Greek food — especially whole lambs and pigs slow-cooked on a spit over an open fire. And hey, preparations are no big deal. One summer, on the Fourth of July (hardly your typical Greek holiday), I saw two Greek families throw up a makeshift sheet metal barbecue pit in the parking lot of their apartment complex, dump 50 pounds of charcoal on the ground, fire that sucker up, and proceed to spit-broil a 100-pound lamb that they'd trussed to a steel rod "borrowed" from a nearby construction site. They had more fun with less fuss than any people I've ever met.

Some popular ingredients: As far as produce goes, let the ingredients in a Greek salad be your guide. They were mentioned above. Greeks are very big on olives, olive oil, wine, wine vinegar, and ouzo. Lots of ouzo. Oregano is as popular in Greek recipes as in Italian ones, and I've seen it sold in 25-pound sacks in Greek grocery stores in Tarpon Springs, Florida, which has more Greeks per square mile than any other city in the country.

Many Greek recipes use lamb, pork, and exotic, tentacled sea creatures, such as octopus and squid, as main ingredients. Some dishes call for grape leaves, which are either stuffed with or wrapped around the ingredients, depending on the recipe. You can buy them in jars in gourmet markets or grow your own in the back yard. Also lay in a supply of garlic, parsley, green peppers, assorted herbs and spices, pignoli (pine nuts), and lemons.

A PARTING WORD

One final suggestion to complement what you've learned so far: be *enthusiastic* about what you've prepared, and let your guests *know* it. Instill in them the notion that they're gonna have one spectacular dinner, and you've got a psychological edge. They're primed for a good experience.

One supersuccessful advertising executive routinely opened his presentations to clients by hollering, "We've got the best damn ad campaign you people have ever seen in your lives! I guarantee you, by the time we're done, you're gonna love our pitch so much you're gonna wet your pants!"

With a slightly different choice of words, you too can convey your absolute conviction about the success of your cooking. People will believe it's going to taste great, and that's half the battle.

Composer Andre Previn, for example, once wanted to adopt a Vietnamese orphan. A woman who had run a Saigon orphanage stayed with the Previn family for a weekend to evaluate their suitability as adoptive parents. When the lady asked for a bowl of cereal for breakfast, Previn reached for the health food cereal his two sons regularly ate. He poured her a generous helping and began extolling the nutritional value of the cereal as she gradually emptied the bowl. "To be quite honest," she admitted, "I'm not crazy about it." Previn looked once more at what he'd served her and answered, "I'm not surprised. I've just made you eat a large dish of hamster food."

But think about it. If mass hysteria can make a cafeteria full of grade schoolers all start barfing in unison, why can't the same power of suggestion work to a positive (and much less messy) end? It's certainly worth a shot.

Take the lead by showing lots of enthusiasm, and your attitude may spread throughout your dinner party before you can say "salmonella." *Tell* them they're going to love the food. Invite them into your kitchen to savor the aromas. Brandish some of your cutlery. Take their temperature with your surface temp thermometer. As they pass beneath your garlands of garlic and hot peppers, make their experience a rite of passage into the magic world of gastronomic gratification. You can all explore it together, because (although they don't know it) you're just one step ahead of them!

Press on, brave leader.

Bon Appétit!

Bluffer's Guides
CENTENNIAL PRESS

The biggest bluff about the *Bluffer's Guides* is the title. These books are full of information — and fun.

NOW IN STOCK — $3.95
Bluffer's Guide to Bluffing
Bluff Your Way in British Theatre
Bluff Your Way in Computers
Bluff Your Way in Hollywood
Bluff Your Way in Japan
Bluff Your Way in Management
Bluff Your Way in Music
Bluff Your Way in the Occult
Bluff Your Way in Paris
Bluff Your Way in Public Speaking

NEW TITLES
Bluff Your Way in Baseball
Bluff Your Way in the Deep South
Bluff Your Way in Football
Bluff Your Way in Golf
Bluff Your Way in Gourmet Cooking
Bluff Your Way in Marketing
Bluff Your Way in New York
Bluff Your Way in Wine

AVAILABLE SOON
Bluff Your Way in Basketball
Bluff Your Way in Office Politics
Bluff Your Way in Dining Out
Bluff Your Way in Fitness
Bluff Your Way in Home Maintenance
Bluff Your Way in Las Vegas
Bluff Your Way in London
Bluff Your Way in Marriage
Bluff Your Way in Parenting
Bluff Your Way in Psychology
Bluff Your Way in Sex

To order any of the Bluffer's Guides titles, use the order form on the next page.

Get Bluffer's Guides at your bookstore or use this order form to send for the copies you want. Send it with your check or money order to:

Centennial Press
Box 82087
Lincoln, NE 68501

Title	Quantity	$3.95 Each
Total Enclosed		

Name_____

Address_____

City _____

State_____ Zip_____